FOLK-SONGS FOR CHOIRS 2

Thirteen arrangements for unaccompanied mixed voices

Edited by John Rutter

Music Department
OXFORD UNIVERSITY PRESS
Oxford and New York

Oxford University Press, Walton Street, Oxford OX2 6DP, England
Oxford University Press, 200 Madison Avenue, New York, NY 10016, USA

Oxford New York Toronto
Delhi Bombay Calcutta Madras Karachi
Petaling Jaya Singapore Hong Kong Tokyo
Nairobi Dar es Salaam Cape Town
Melbourne Auckland

and associated companies in
Berlin Ibadan

Oxford is a trade mark of Oxford University Press

Folk-songs for Choirs 2 gathers together into a single volume thirteen unaccompanied mixed-voice arrangements of folk-songs from the British Isles. Several of the settings, such as Percy Grainger's *Brigg Fair* and Vaughan Williams's *The turtle dove*, have long been regarded as classics of their kind but have been available only as separate leaflets; others equally fine, such as Bairstow's *The oak and the ash*, are no longer in print and are here revived after some years of neglect. *Afton Water*, arranged by Sir David Willcocks, appears in print for the first time, and John Byrt's settings of *Faithful Johnny* and *The keel row* were specially commissioned for this collection.

The companion volume *Folk-songs for Choirs 1* contains twelve unaccompanied mixed-voice arrangements of songs from the British Isles and North America.

Contents

for Robert Tear, FRCM

1. AFTON WATER

Words by
ROBERT BURNS

Scottish folk-song
arranged by
DAVID WILLCOCKS

*One or more of these verses may be sung by a solo voice with humming choir.

VERSES 2 and 4

DESCANT (ALTOS or BASSES)

Ah_____ Ah___

MELODY (SOPRANOS or TENORS)

2. How lof - ty, sweet Af - ton, thy_ neigh-bour-ing_ hills,_Far mark'd with the_
4. Thy cry-stal stream, Af - ton, how_ love - ly it _ glides And winds by the_

Ah_____

cours - es of_ clear-wind-ing_ rills! There dai - ly I_ wan - der as
cot where my_ Ma - ry_ re - sides! How wan - ton_ thy_ wa - ters her

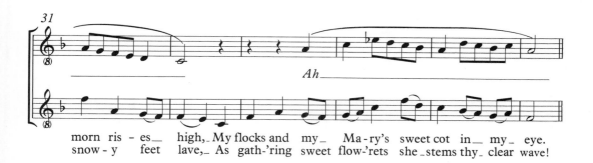

Ah_____

morn ris - es_ high,_My flocks and my_ Ma - ry's sweet cot in_ my_ eye.
snow - y feet lave,_ As gath'-ring sweet flow'-rets she _stems thy_ clear wave!

37 CODA

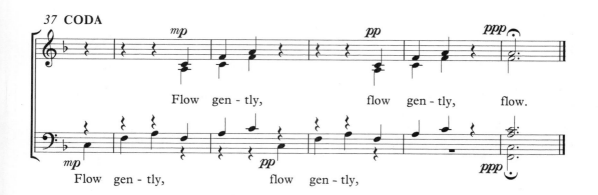

mp *pp* *ppp*

Flow gen - tly, flow gen - tly, flow.

mp *pp* *ppp*

Flow gen - tly, flow gen - tly,

lovingly and reverently dedicated to the memory of Edvard Grieg

2. BRIGG FAIR

Lincolnshire folk-song
collected and arranged by
PERCY GRAINGER

1. It was on the fifth of Au-gust, *er the wea-ther
(2.) up with the lark in the morn-ing, with my heart so

fine and fair,___ un-to Brigg Fair I did re-pair, for
full of glee,___ of think-ing there to meet my dear,_ long

*Er is a folk-singer's nonsense-syllable and should rhyme with *her* (the 'r' being mute).

© Schott & Co., London, 1911 Reprinted by permission

3. CA' THE YOWES

Words by
ROBERT BURNS

Scottish folk-song
arranged by
R. VAUGHAN WILLIAMS

lift sae hie Till death_ shall blin' my e'e_____ Ye shall be my

lift sae hie Till clay - cauld death shall blin' my e'e Ye shall be my

lift sae hie Till death_ shall blin' my e'e_____ Ye shall be my

lift sae hie Till death shall blin' my e'e Ye shall be my

TENOR SOLO

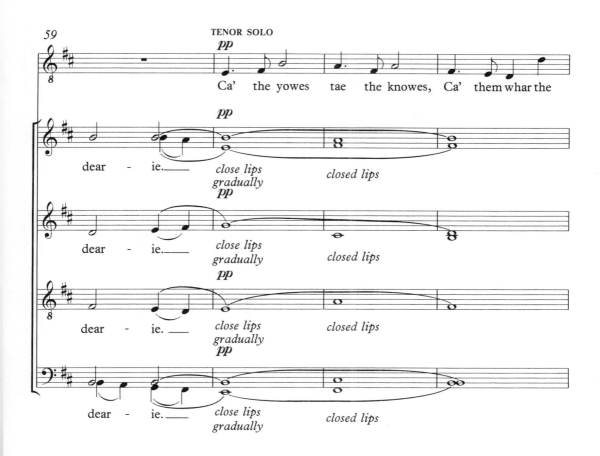

Ca' the yowes tae the knowes, Ca' them whar the

dear - ie._ *close lips gradually* *closed lips*

dear - ie._ *close lips gradually* *closed lips*

dear - ie. _ *close lips gradually* *closed lips*

dear - ie._ *close lips gradually*

4. FAITHFUL JOHNNY

Scottish traditional song
arranged by
JOHN BYRT

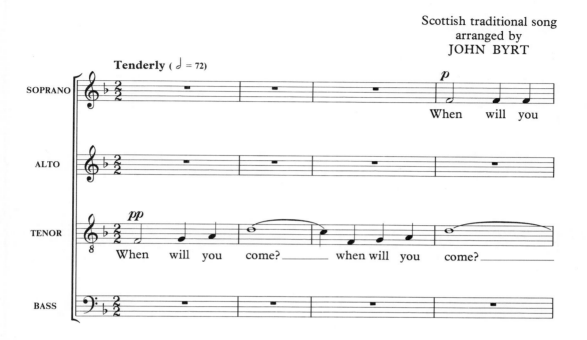

5. I LOVE MY LOVE

Cornish folk-song
collected by G. B. Gardiner
arranged by G. HOLST

17

pa - rents

cru - el__ were his pa - rents who__ sent my love to sea, And__

pa - rents

pa - rents

21

ship__ that bore my__ love from me;

cru - el__ was__ the ship__ that__ bore my love from me; Yet I

25

I

love his__ pa-rents since they're his al - though they've ruin-ed me;

love my love be - cause I know my__ love loves me!"

29

pp

I

(closed lips)

33

sotto voce

S.   love my love, I love my love, love my love, I love my love,

sotto voce

A.   love my love, I love my love, love my love, I love my love,

p affettuoso

T.

3. "With straw I'll__ weave a gar - land, I'll__

love my love, I love my love, love my love, I love my

love my love, I love my love, love my love, I __ love my

weave it ve - ry fine; With ro - ses, __ li - lies, dai - sies, I'll

love be-cause I know, __

love be-cause I know, __

mix the __ eg - lan - tine; And I'll pre - sent it to my love when

be - cause I know my love loves me. For I love my love be-

be - cause I know my __ love loves me. For I love my love be-

he re - turns from sea. For I love my love, be - cause I know my __

6. STRAWBERRY FAIR

West country folk-song
arranged by
DONALD JAMES

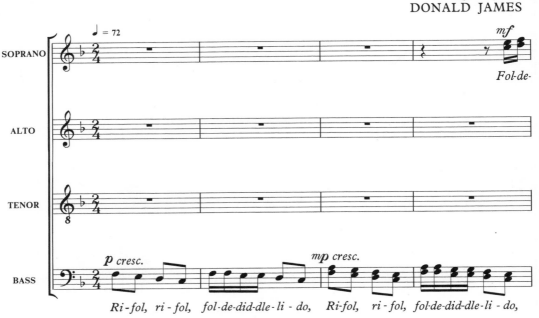

to C.K.S. and the Oriana

7. SWANSEA TOWN

Folk-song
collected by
G. B. Gardiner
arranged by
G. HOLST

Allegro moderato

TENOR
and
BASS

Oh! fare-well to you my Nan-cy, ten thou-sand times a-

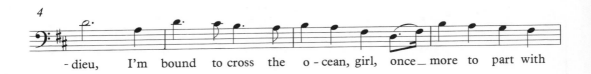

-dieu, I'm bound to cross the o-cean, girl, once_more to part with

you; Once more to part from you, fine girl, you're the girl that I a-

-dore, But still I live in hopes to see old_Swan-sea Town once_

Old_Swan-sea

S.
A.

Old_Swan - sea Town once more, fine_ girl,_____

more. Old_Swan-sea Town_____ once_ more, fine girl, you're the

T.
B.

more. Old_Swan-sea Town

8. THE KEEL ROW

Tyneside traditional song
arranged by
JOHN BYRT

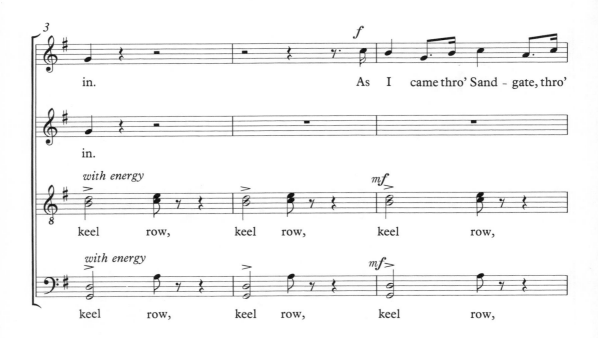

9. THE OAK AND THE ASH

Old English air
arranged by
EDWARD BAIRSTOW

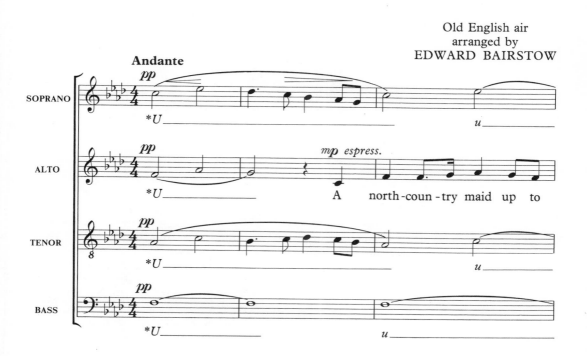

*Humming with the lips very slightly parted. Approximately the sound of 'u' in 'murmur'.

© Oxford University Press 1928

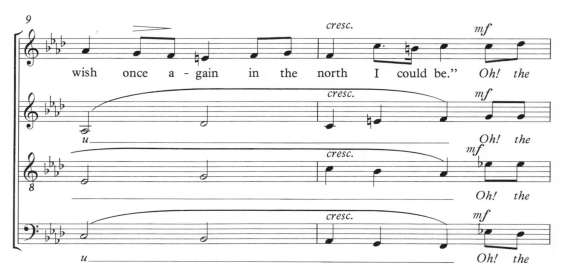

30

No___doubt did I please I could mar - ry at ease; Where

33

cresc.

maid-ens are fair___ ma-ny lov-ers will come; But___ he whom I wed must be

cresc.

36

f

north-coun-try bred, And___car-ry me back to my north-coun-try home: *Oh! the*

f

39

dim.

oak, and the ash, and the bon-ny i - vy tree,___ They flou - rish at home in my

f

Oh! the oak, and the ash, and the bon-ny i - vy tree, *dim.* *At home in my*

42

Lento

poco rit.   *pp*

p

own coun - try. They flou - rish at home in my own coun - try.

pp

own coun - try.

for T. B. Lawrence and the Fleet Street Choir

10. THE SAILOR AND YOUNG NANCY

Norfolk folk-song
collected and arranged by
E. J. MOERAN

11. THE THREE RAVENS

Traditional ballad
arranged by
EDWARD T. CHAPMAN

12. THE TURTLE DOVE

English folk-song
collected and arranged by
R. VAUGHAN WILLIAMS

The sea will nev-er run dry, Nor the rocks melt with the

The sea will nev-er run dry, my dear, Nor the rocks nev-er melt with the

The sea will nev-er run dry, my dear, Nor the rocks melt with the

The sea will nev-er run dry, my dear, Nor the rocks nev-er melt with the

The sea will nev-er run dry, my dear, Nor the rocks nev-er melt with the

sun, But I nev - - er will prove false, Till

sun, But I nev-er will prove false to the bon-ny lass I love, Till

sun, But I nev - - er will prove false, Till

sun, But I nev-er will prove false to the bon-ny lass I love, Till

sun, But I nev - - er will prove false, Till

all be done, my dear, Till all these things be done.

all these things be done, my dear, Till all these things be done.

all be done, my dear, Till all these things be done.

all these things be done, my dear, Till all these things be done.

all these things be done, my dear, Till all these things be done.

BAR. SOLO: O yon-der doth sit that lit-tle tur-tle dove, He doth sit on yon-der high

S. *(closed lips)*

A. *(closed lips)*

T. *(closed lips)*

B. *(closed lips)*

tree,   A - mak-ing a moan for the loss of his love, As _ I will do for

(s.1 *half closed lips*)

thee, my dear, As _ I will do for thee._____

(*closed lips*)

13. YARMOUTH FAIR

Words by
HAL COLLINS

Norfolk folk-tune
arranged by PETER WARLOCK
adapted by C. ARMSTRONG GIBBS

Available separately (X 37). Also available in the following forms: (a) Solo song (b) Unison song with simplified accompaniment [OCS U 14] (c) Two-part song arranged by C. Armstrong Gibbs [OCS T 23].

Processed and printed by
Halstan & Co. Ltd., Amersham, Bucks., England